LIVING IN
CHINA

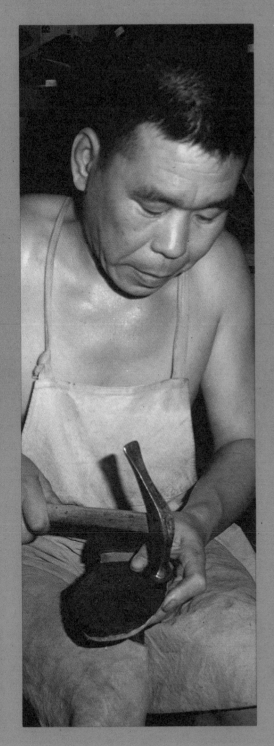

LIVING IN
CHINA

Edna Bakken

Eric Domke

General Editor
Dr. Edward E. Owen

The Book Society of Canada Limited
Agincourt Canada

ISBN 0-7725-5265-7

Canadian Cataloguing in Publication Data

Bakken, Edna.
   Living in China

For use in elementary schools.

ISBN 0-7725-5265-7

1. China–Social Conditions–1976–
I. Domke, Eric Douglas, 1935–　II. Owen, Edward E.　III. Title.

HN733.5.B34　　　　　　　951.05′7　　　　　　　C82-095231-1

Photo Credits

Len Sampson, i, ii (left and centre), viii (top and bottom right), ix (bottom left), 7 (top), 8, 10 (bottom), 13, 14, 15, 16 (top right), 17, 19, 20, 22, 24, 29, 31, 33, 37 (bottom), 44 (right), 50, 56, 58, 59, 60, 62, 63, 64, 65, 66, 67 (right), 70, 76, 77, 82, 84

Edward E. Owen, ii (right), iii, viii (top and bottom left), ix (top left and right and bottom right), 3, 4, 6, 10 (top), 12, 16 (left and bottom right), 23, 28, 34, 35, 37 (top), 40, 41, 42, 43, 44 (left), 45, 46, 47 (top), 51, 53, 54, 57, 61, 67 (left), 68, 69, 71, 72, 73, 74, 80, 81, 85

V. Falkenheim, 55, 78, 79

British Columbia Hydro, 47 (bottom)

Developed by Clare Educational Development Inc.

Text and cover design/Robert Burgess Garbutt
Editing/Kahn and Associates
Maps/Sam Daniel
Typesetting/ART-U Graphics Ltd.
Colour separations/Offset Film Ltd.
Printed and bound in Canada by Bryant Press Limited

2 3 4 5 6 7 8 BP 90 89 88 87 86 85 84 83

Contents

Introduction

Canada and China are large countries. Almost all of Canada lies north of the 49th parallel of latitude (49°N). Most of China lies between 20°N and 50°N.

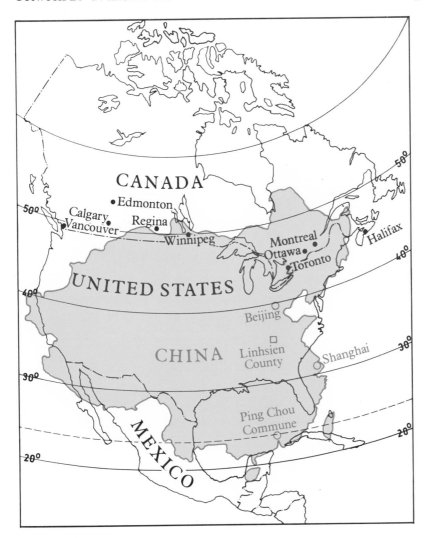

Here, a map of China has been placed across a map of North America, in the correct *latitudes*.

As you can see, most of China lies south of Canada in the same latitudes as the United States. The southern areas of China are in the same latitudes as Mexico.

The places we will study in this book are marked on the map of China.

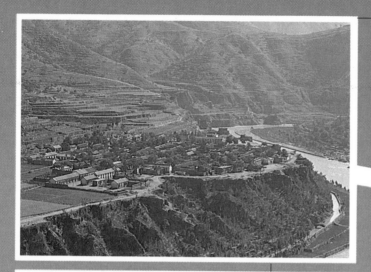

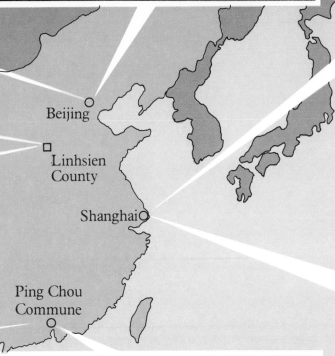

Beijing

Linhsien
County

Shanghai

Ping Chou
Commune

How to Use This Book

This book is about China and its people. It tells how they live and work on the land or in the cities. The book is divided into four chapters.

The first chapter tells the story of a family in Ping Chou Commune in southern China. The commune grows rice in the hot, moist climate at the mouth of the Pearl River. The chapter describes how the commune organization works.

The next chapter deals with the way the people in a poor area changed their lives. The people live in a county in a mountainous area in central China. They built a canal through the mountains to bring water to their land. Their story is one of courage and endurance in the face of great hardship.

The third chapter is about Shanghai, the largest city in China. A neighbourhood community is studied. As well, the factories and services in the city are described.

The final chapter is about China's capital, Beijing, in northern China. A brief account of China's long history is included. Read this chapter first if you want to learn a little bit about the history and government of China. Since this book is mainly about how people live in China, the last chapter is very short. If you want to know more about China's government or history, visit your school or public library. There you will find many books that will help you.

The many pictures, maps, charts, and graphs in the book tell their own story. The questions with the illustrations should help you understand China and its people. References to Canada will help to show the differences and similarities between the two countries.

Difficult or technical words are included in a glossary at the end of the book. Use it, as well as your dictionary, to find out the meaning of any words that you do not understand.

1 Ping Chou Commune

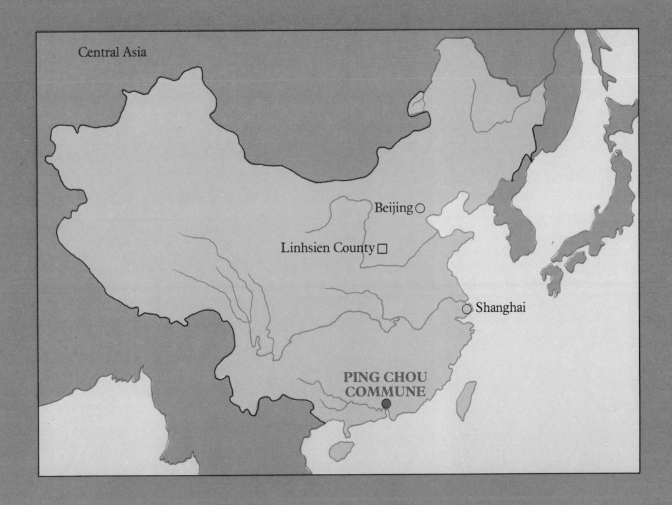

Central Asia

Beijing ○

Linhsien County □

○ Shanghai

PING CHOU COMMUNE ●

What a Commune Is

In rural China people live in communes. All communes are different. They differ in size, population, and the goods they produce. All of them produce food, because communes are mainly organizations of farming communities. What they produce depends on where they are located, on the climate and soil, and on what the land surface is like. Some grow rice, others wheat or other grains. All of them grow vegetables, and most of them grow fruit. Some communes specialize in growing cotton or tea. Almost everywhere you will find animals, particularly pigs, ducks, and chickens.

All communes have factories. They make all kinds of goods mainly to supply their own needs—clothing, shoes, bricks, baskets, farm tools, bicycles, and so on.

When communes have extra goods, they sell them to other communes or to the government. The money received is used to buy goods they do not produce themselves.

List some ways in which this basket factory differs from a Canadian factory.

Communes did not appear overnight. They developed over several years. The Communist party came to power in China in 1949. But communes did not begin until 1958. The following chart shows how communes developed.

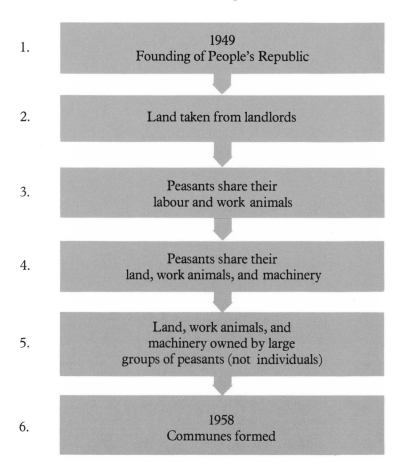

1. 1949
Founding of People's Republic

2. Land taken from landlords

3. Peasants share their
labour and work animals

4. Peasants share their
land, work animals, and machinery

5. Land, work animals, and
machinery owned by large
groups of peasants (not individuals)

6. 1958
Communes formed

As you can see, after 1949 the land was taken from the landlords by the government. It was then divided among the peasants. At stage 3 in the chart the land was still privately owned. But now the peasants exchanged their labour and work animals to help each other.

In stage 4 the land, work animals, and machinery were shared. The peasants received wages for the work they did. They also

Ping Chou Commune is near the coast in southeast China. The climate is warm in winter and hot in summer. In winter dry winds blow from central Asia across China. In summer winds blow from the Pacific Ocean. These winds bring rain.

The climate in Ping Chou is called *monsoon* because the winds blow from opposite directions in winter and summer. Look at a map in an atlas to see that this is true.

Look at the climate graph for Ping Chou Commune.

- Which are the four wettest months? What are the temperatures in those months?
- Which are the two driest months? How much rain is there then?
- What is the climate like in your area? How is it different from the climate in Ping Chou Commune?

Climate Graph for Ping Chou Commune

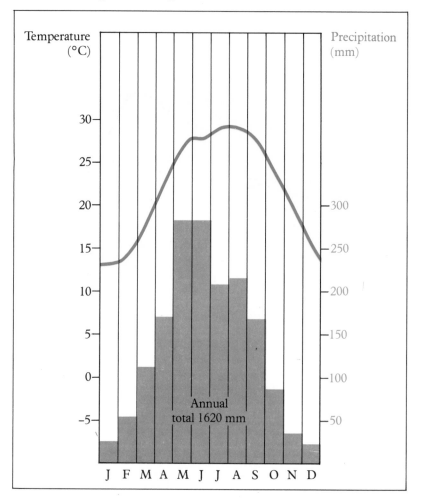

received a share of the profits when the crops were sold. In stage 5 the land, animals, and machinery were owned by an advanced co-operative (a central organization). The peasants were paid wages for the work they did.

In 1958 the co-operatives banded together to form people's communes. Now industry as well as farming was owned by the commune. Communes replaced the local government. They organized the working and social life of the people.

Commune Organization

The commune is organized on three levels. The three levels of the
Ping Chou Commune are shown in this chart.

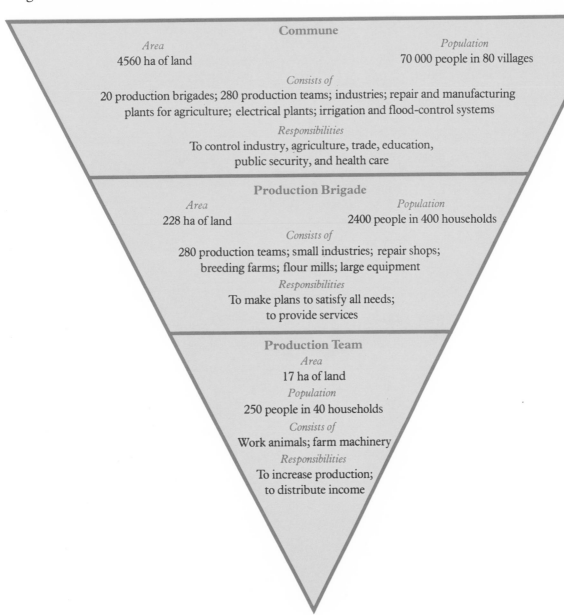

Commune

Area
4560 ha of land

Population
70 000 people in 80 villages

Consists of
20 production brigades; 280 production teams; industries; repair and manufacturing
plants for agriculture; electrical plants; irrigation and flood-control systems

Responsibilities
To control industry, agriculture, trade, education,
public security, and health care

Production Brigade

Area
228 ha of land

Population
2400 people in 400 households

Consists of
280 production teams; small industries; repair shops;
breeding farms; flour mills; large equipment

Responsibilities
To make plans to satisfy all needs;
to provide services

Production Team
Area
17 ha of land
Population
250 people in 40 households
Consists of
Work animals; farm machinery
Responsibilities
To increase production;
to distribute income

The Chan Family

The Chan family lives in Tung Tsuen village on the Ping Chou Commune, twenty kilometres from the city of Guangzhou. All the land is flat and used for growing rice. In the hot, moist climate two crops are grown each year. In addition pigs, geese, ducks, chickens, dairy cows, and fish are raised.

The Chan family consists of a son, Chan Kwok Ming, who is thirteen years old, and a daughter, Chan Yu Chu, who is twelve. Here they play the *p'i p'a,* which is played like a guitar. They practise with other children in the village recreation hall.

Their father, Chan Ming Tak. He is a cadre on the brigade management committee and also a member of the rice field work team. In this picture Mr. Chan is helping to fit a driving belt on a threshing machine.

Their mother, Chan Leung Siu Ying. She works in a small basket factory that is run by the production brigade. Before she married Mr. Chan, her surname was "Leung". When she married Mr. Chan, she added "Chan" to her name.

Their grandfather, Chan Chi Ching, aged 61. He has retired from work on the commune. He helps with feeding the animals and gardening.

Their grandmother, Chan Wong Pui Yee, aged 56. She helps in the day-care centre. She and Grandfather Chan live next door to Chan Ming Tak with another of their sons.

The Chans' Home

Mr. and Mrs. Chan and their two children live in a one-storey brick house that they built for themselves. Mr. Chan borrowed 400 yuan from the brigade to buy the roof tiles, brick, and mortar. Chu and Ming helped mix and carry mortar, while Mr. and Mrs. Chan laid the bricks. It took a long time to build the Chan home, but everyone was happy to move into the clean, dry building.

Plan of the Chan Home

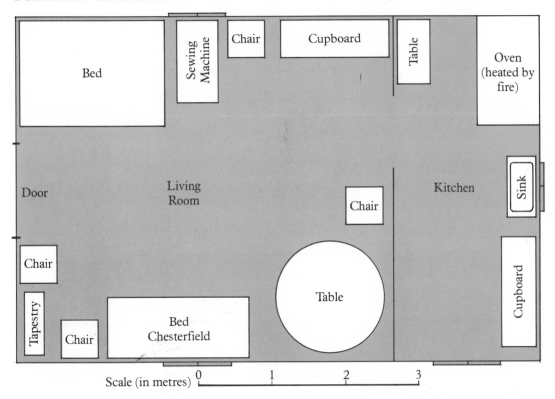

Scale (in metres) 0 1 2 3

In each house there is only enough electricity for one light bulb. There is no other power in the Chan home. They use twigs and straw for fuel for the oven in the kitchen.

Imagine what it would be like in your home with no power.

How would your family cook meals, wash clothes, and heat the house? What would everyone do in the evening?

Draw a plan of your own living room to the same scale (2 cm : 1 m) as this plan.

Imagine that four people are living, eating, and sleeping in that space. What problems would they have to face? How would your life be different if you had to live as the Chan family does?

These pictures show the inside and outside of the Chan home.

Mrs. Chan makes clothes for her family. She was pleased when she had enough money to buy a sewing machine. Most families want to own a sewing machine. Why do you think that Grandmother was also delighted when she first saw it?

Mr. and Mrs. Chan sleep on the bed that you see in the picture. There is a mosquito net hanging on the wall. How and why is it used?

How can you tell from the picture that the weather is hot?

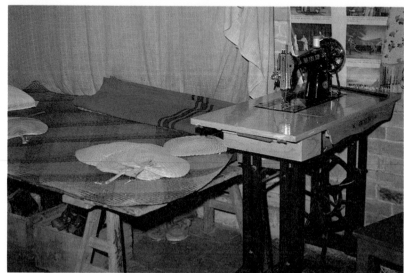

Mr. Chan and his two brothers built their homes close together so that they could combine their own gardens and grow more vegetables. The three Chan families do not own this land. But they are allowed to build their homes and grow food on it.

Site of the Homes of the Three Chan Families

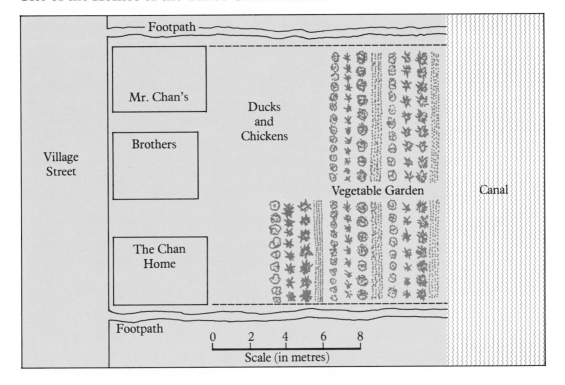

Look at the plan above. It shows the homes of the three Chan brothers.
- What is the size of a building lot in your neighbourhood?
- Draw a plan of a Canadian lot to the same scale as the site plan (1 cm : 2 m).
- Compare your drawing with the plan below.
- Who has more land?

- What might a Canadian family grow on its lot?
- Is it better to grow your own vegetables or to buy them from the store? Why?

The street in front of the houses of the three Chan families leads into the centre of Tung Tsuen. The houses in the village are close together with only a footpath between them. About 170 families live here. The population of the village is about 900. In Tung Tsuen there are two stores, a basket factory, a school, a repair shop

Tung Tsuen village

for bicycles, a small health clinic, a storehouse for rice, and a recreation hall.

There is a canal behind the Chans' house. It is one of hundreds that help control flooding at the mouth of the Pearl River.

Find the Pearl River in your atlas. It is the largest river in southern China. The boat you see is called a *sampan*.
- What are the steps for? What is the sampan used for? Why is the canal like a roadway?

- Imagine your community without cars, buses, and trucks. Life would be very different for the people.
- How would you get downtown?

- How would your family get to work? Buy the groceries?
- Why would the streets have to be shorter?
- How would people move heavy loads around?

How the Chans Earn Their Living

Everyone in the Chan household shares the work. As well, both Mr. and Mrs. Chan work outside the home to earn money.

Mr. Chan has two jobs. He is a cadre, which is a member of the brigade management committee. He also works in the rice fields. The committee chooses which crops the brigade will grow and

Ploughing

Although more and more machines are being used on the commune, some buffalo are still used for ploughing. After the ploughing, the seedlings are planted. As the rice is growing, weeding and fertilizing have to be done. At harvest time as many people as possible help to cut the rice, thresh it on the simple machines, and carry it away to the drying area. The rice stalks are then taken to a small factory to be cut up for animal food.

When the commune gets tractors for ploughing, planting, and harvesting—and some are in use now—how will this affect Mr. Chan's life and work?

Planting seedlings

what machinery it will buy. The cadres decide how the brigade can become more self-sufficient and how it will grow the amount of rice the commune asks for each year. Six days of the week Mr. Chan works in the rice fields. His special job is looking after the machinery. For this he earns work points. His wage is based on these work points. If he does extra work, he earns extra work points.

Fertilizing

Harvesting and threshing

Rice-drying area

Making basket sides

Weaving baskets   Carting baskets

Mrs. Chan works in the village basket factory. She weaves cane baskets. While her fingers are busy weaving, Mrs. Chan talks to the other workers. Mrs. Chan starts work at 8:00 in the morning. She arrives home before her husband returns from the rice fields at sundown. Some of the money she earns is used to buy extras such as cloth, dishes, curtains, and mats for her home.

The basket factory is small and very little machinery is used. Nearly all the workers are married women. The baskets they make are used for carrying rice or vegetables. They are taken by sampan or cart to other villages and to Guangzhou, where they are sold. Why is it important for the commune to provide work for women?

The Chans do not have to spend much money to meet their basic needs. Much of their food is provided by the commune or grown in their own garden. Each year the family is given a share of rice. If Mr. and Mrs. Chan earn extra work points, the amount of rice they are given is increased. The family grows many of its own vegetables, raises ducks, chickens, and pigs, and catches fish and shrimp in the canal. The Chans buy beef, fruit, tea, and some pork and vegetables. Mrs. Chan buys cotton cloth to make the family's clothing. The family's shoes are bought at the village store.

The Chans may shop in Guangzhou, in the village store, or at a roadside stand.

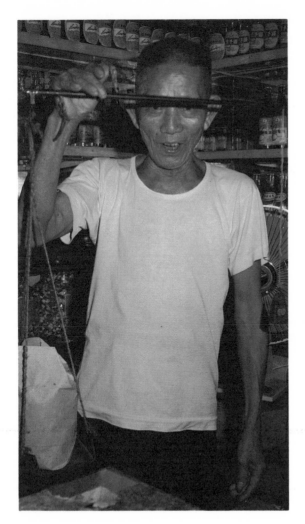

Chan Family Earnings Per Month

Mr. Chan	40 yuan
Mrs. Chan	35 yuan
Vegetable sales	10 yuan
Total	85 yuan

Chan Family Expenses Per Month

Food	35 yuan
Clothing	10 yuan
Electricity	3 yuan
Home loan repayment	5 yuan
Medical	20 fen*
Extras	17 yuan
Savings	about 14.80 yuan

*1 yuan = 100 fen

Some Average Prices

Bicycle	150 yuan	Cloth shoes	4 yuan
Sewing machine	200 yuan	Plastic shoes	2 yuan
Watch	100 yuan	Pork (per kilogram)	2 yuan
Thermos flask	8 yuan	Beef (per kilogram)	2 yuan
Metal bucket	6 yuan	Fruit (per kilogram)	1-2 yuan
Cotton cloth* (per metre)	1 yuan	Tea (per kilogram)	2 yuan
Television set	400-1200 yuan	Eggs (per kilogram)	2 yuan
Mosquito net	6 yuan		
Wool blanket	60 yuan		
Wok	2 yuan		
Dinner set for six	20 yuan		

*Each person is allowed to buy six metres of cotton cloth per year.

Look at the prices in the list.

• How long did Mr. Chan have to work to buy the new sewing machine?

• Next year Ming will go to secondary school in the next village and will need a bicycle to get there. About how long will Mrs. Chan have to work to buy one?

• Why do you think bicycles, sewing machines, and television sets are expensive?

• What are the big differences between the expenses of the Chan family and the expenses of your family? Explain them.

Sometimes Mr. Chan fishes with his friends in a large fish pond near the village. They share the catch.

Ming is raising some goats. He will sell them to the commune to help with the family income.

Grandfather and Grandmother Remember the Past

Grandfather Chan spends much of his time working in the garden or tending the rabbits, ducks, chickens, and pigs. Every day he waters plants, feeds the livestock, cleans cages, and gathers vegetables and eggs for the tables of the three Chan families. Whenever the garden needs it, he weeds and fertilizes the plants. Grandfather Chan calls the pigs and chickens his "little fertilizer factories". One of the pigs belongs to all three families. The other one will be sold to buy a bicycle for Ming's daily journey to secondary school next year. When there are extra vegetables, they are sold and the money is shared among the three Chan families.

Chu and Ming often help Grandfather Chan with the weeding. Sometimes he tells them stories of the days when he was a boy. Even though they have heard the same stories many times, the children listen politely. This is one he tells most often:

> Grandchildren, you are so lucky to have enough to eat, a
> warm place to sleep, and nice clothes to wear. When I was a

Grandfather Chan has been carrying loads on shoulder poles all his life. Ming admires him because he can do many things. Grandfather does much of the work in the Chans' garden. Grandfather and Grandmother both receive small pensions from the commune. As well, their children help to take care of them.

boy, I was always hungry. There was never enough rice for our family of six, even though my father worked for a very rich landlord. It was an event to celebrate if we caught a fish to go with our rice.

One year my father did not have rice for seed. He had to borrow from the landlord. But the crops did not do well, and he could not repay the debt. The next year we were even further in debt and hungrier still. Finally, my father sold one of my sisters so that the family would not starve. I never saw her again. She may still be alive. I do not know. Soon afterwards, I ran away to Guangzhou, or Canton as it was called then. I have never been able to find any of my family since then.

Weed vigorously, little Chu. We must grow vegetables for everyone. Life is good. We are lucky to have so much.

Grandmother Chan, too, has stories to tell. When Ming and Chu complain about their homework and chores, she reminds them of how fortunate they are to live now rather than when she was a girl. This is Grandmother Chan's story:

When I was a girl, we lived in a straw hut. When it rained outside, it rained inside! My Grandmother Wong's word was law. We did as we were told without question, even when she made my sister and me do all the housework as well as work in the fields.

I had no say when it came time to marry your Grandfather Chan. It was arranged before I knew anything about it. I was only fifteen years old when I got married, but then no one waited until they were twenty-five or older as people do now. I had five children to care for by the time I was twenty-one years old. There was no time for basketball games, plays, music, movies, or television—all the things that you enjoy.

You are so fortunate to be able to learn to read and write. Especially you, Chu. It was unheard of to educate girls when I was young. Study hard, my children. Make the family proud of you. Make China proud of you.

Cooking for the Chan families when they all get together is a big job. Sometimes twenty people sit down for a meal.

- Can you tell what they are eating?
- What might be in the small bowls?
- What are the spoons for?

Grandmother Chan is up by 5:00 each morning to start a fire with rice straw in the adobe and brick stove. When the stove gets hot, she puts the woks into the special wells made for them in the stove top. She cooks rice porridge and a vegetable dish of beans and tomatoes and makes tea for the family's breakfast. Grandmother fills the thermos flasks with boiling water so that she can make tea when friends drop in to visit. Three afternoons a week, Grandmother Chan helps in the day-care centre. She is not paid a wage for this. When Chu and Ming were younger, Grandmother cared for them at home. They do not need her care as much now that they are older.

Grandmother Chan enjoys having the three Chan families together to celebrate special occasions. She cooks many delicious dishes for a birthday, the Spring Festival (Lunar New Year), or National Day on October 1. But best of all, family gatherings are a good time to tell stories.

The Chan Children

The Chan children go to the commune school in Tung Tsuen village. They study Chinese, mathematics, science, English, physical education, and music. All of the older children take turns cleaning the school and playground.

Ming is one year ahead of Chu. He hopes to attend the agricultural college that the commune has just built. Chu studies hard so that when her turn comes she may also go to secondary school. She would like to become a doctor or a nurse in the commune hospital.

At home Chu is learning to embroider with silk thread. Her uncle got the thread in Guangzhou on one of his many trips down

Children do exercises before they go to classes in the morning. They march in to a marching tune played over the loudspeakers. Classes are large: often there are fifty students to a class.

Chu working on her embroidery

The school often puts on plays in ▶
the village. The children love to
dress up and act out parts,
particularly when there are
"good guys" and "bad guys" in
the play.

the canals in his sampan. Grandmother Chan is teaching Chu to make neat, even stitches. When her work is finished, it will be sent to the commune workshop to be sold. Chu will get some of the money from the sale.

Chu and Ming help Uncle Wu, a senior citizen, with his chores. Uncle Wu is not really their uncle. But because he has no family, the brigade committee chose the Chan children to help him. The commune promises orphans and old people who have no families five things. These are food, clothing, shelter, medical care, and a decent burial.

Every day, before and after school, the children stop at Uncle Wu's. Chu usually cooks and shops while Ming cleans and carries water from the tap at the end of the street. Ming often walks with Uncle Wu to the evening basketball games in the schoolyard or takes him to the recreation hall whenever there is entertainment there. The older people are always given the best seats in the hall. Plays are a favourite entertainment for Uncle Wu. Sometimes he misses a movie or a musical, but he never misses a play.

2 The Red Flag Canal in Linhsien County

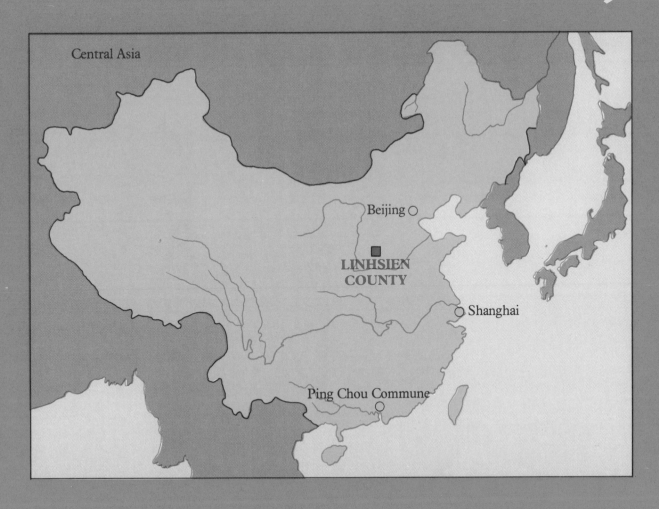

Central Asia

Beijing ○

■
LINHSIEN
COUNTY

○ Shanghai

Ping Chou Commune
○

Solving the Problem of Drought

Linhsien County is in Central China. It is a mountainous place, but there are valleys and plains between the mountain ranges. The climate is cold and dry in winter and hot and wet in summer. Three rivers flow across the county. When the rains do not come, the rivers dry up. Sometimes the rain falls very heavily. This causes serious floods. For centuries the peasants were miserable because they had to live with droughts and floods.

Climate Graph for Linhsien County

Look at the climate graph for Linhsien. Like Ping Chou Commune the climate is dry in winter and wet in summer. But at Linhsien the summer rains are much lighter. Linhsien is very far inland. In summer the rain winds from the Pacific lose much of their moisture as they move inland.

Compare this climate graph with the one in chapter 1 for Ping Chou Commune.

- What is the difference in annual *precipitation* between Linhsien and Ping Chou Commune?
- How many months are below freezing (0°C) in Linhsien?
- Is the climate in your area like the climate in Linhsien? Explain.

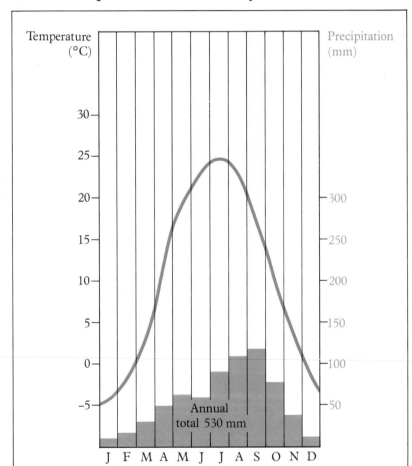

You can see from this map that Linhsien County has mountains on all sides. In the centre are plains and valleys.

河北省

山西省

KEY

Communes ★

Rivers —

0 5 10 15

Kilometres

林县水利建设示意图

The rivers that flow across the county often run dry because of lack of rain. The land needs water. Many parts of China are like Linhsien County.

At the top of the map (in the north) is the big Changho River. It flows all year round. Between the Changho River and the plains are the high Taihang Mountains.

Can you see how the communes are spread over the county? In order to begin work on the main canal, the peasants had to walk to the Taihang Mountains.

About how far did the peasants in the villages in the south have to walk? How long might it have taken them?

Look carefully at these pictures. The first picture is of a life-size model·of a peasant and his children. The picture was taken in a museum. The second picture was taken some years ago. The workers are building a wall at the entrance to a tunnel. The men in the distance drilling into the cliffs are blasting away the rock to make way for the canal you see on the opposite page. The third picture shows a canal, which must have taken a long time to build, winding along the steep mountainside. In the last picture vegetables are on display at a roadside market. A regular water supply has made possible bumper crops of all kinds of food.

What is the story behind the pictures?

During times of drought the peasants had to carry water many kilometres on shoulder poles to their homes. Years ago the peasants sang this popular song:

> *When there's drought we long for rain.*
> *But then at last when the rains come,*
> *They wash the topsoil from our fields,*
> *Leaving behind just rocks and sand.*

The peasants had no money to build reservoirs to store water for use in dry periods. All the wells were owned by a very few rich people. The nearest big river was many kilometres away over the Taihang Mountains.

When a new government came into power in China in 1949, many changes occurred in the country. Peasants organized into small groups to share their tools and machinery and help each other. They dug large ponds to store water, but these dried up when there was no rain. The peasants formed bigger groups, built larger ponds, and dug deep wells. In the dry season even these dried up.

As you saw in the last chapter, the peasants had formed themselves into communes by 1958. In each commune there were tens of thousands of peasants. With so many workers available, the communes built three big reservoirs and thirty small ones on the three rivers in Linhsien County. But the following year there was a severe drought, and the rivers dried up once more. The peasants realized that if they wanted a regular supply of water they would have to go to the Changho River, which flows all year long. To use the Changho, they would have to build a canal through the Taihang Mountains.

The people of Linhsien County had very little money and no machinery. They were poor, but they were used to hard work. They drew up a plan. Everyone would do something, no matter how little. There would be all kinds of jobs to do, because they had no machinery. After the rocks were blasted with dynamite, thousands of workers would be needed to move the rubble. Hundreds of stonemasons would be needed to quarry the stone for the walls of the canal. Blacksmiths would have to make chisels and sledgehammers. Carpenters would be needed to keep the wooden carts and barrows in good working order. Cooks would have to prepare food for the workers. Children could help by carrying loads and running messages. Those not working on the canal could send food and supplies.

Changing the Land

In 1960 the plan was set in motion. From each of the fourteen communes in the county came hundreds of workers. They had to walk into the Taihang Mountains carrying their belongings. They brought their own shoulder poles, baskets, hammers, drilling rods, chisels, shovels, and other tools. There were few villages in the mountains, so they had to build camps. Food was brought to them in pushcarts because there were no trucks or roads.

The workers first built a dam on the Changho River so they could channel off the water. Then they started to blast the cliffs of the Taihang Mountains. Over 30 000 workers toiled away to build a canal 70 km long, 8 m wide, and 4.3 m deep. It took them over five years to do it. They called this work "fighting the cliffs".

When the main Red Flag Canal was completed, a regular water supply had at last reached Linhsien County. But much work had yet to be done to take the water to the villages and farmland. The main canal was divided into three smaller canals by the use of a diversion lock. From each canal hundreds of channels were built to take the water to the fields.

The land had to be terraced so that as much of it as possible could be used for crops. The water was used again and again as it moved from terrace to terrace. The peasants had to build aqueduct bridges to carry the water across deep gorges. Tunnels had to be cut through hills. Culverts were made to take the water across roads. Sluice gates were installed to control the flow.

It took ten years to complete the work. The Linhsien workers handled enough rock and earth to build a wall 2 m high and 1 m wide from Vancouver to Halifax.

The Taihang Mountains are high. There are many cliffs. The workers had to cut into the cliffs to make a way for the canal. With heavy hammers and steel rods they drilled holes in the hard rock. Then they rammed dynamite into the holes and exploded it.

Some of the cliffs were very steep. Men were lowered on ropes down the cliff face. They hammered and drilled and blasted, again and again. Altogether they cut into fifty cliff faces. Finally, a route was made for the canal. People made up songs and plays about "fighting the cliffs".

- Are the workers working alone or in teams?
- Why is it important to work together when drilling like this?
- Do you see any clothing or tools that drillers in Canada might use?
- What dangers do these workers face?
- Compare the methods used here to those used in building the CPR in Canada. Did railway builders in Canada face the same problems? Explain.

The canal was lined with blocks of stone. Each stone block was chipped by hand and carried up the cliffs. Mortar, which is used to cement blocks together, had to be made and also carried up to the builders. The workers had no machinery to help them. Men and women worked together carrying the loads. They knew they had to build a good strong wall to hold the water. In some places the cliffs towered above the canal.

- Why do you think the water is the colour it is?
- Why did the workers make a footpath on the canal wall?
- What machinery would have been most useful to the workers?
- The canal would always need to be kept in good repair. What might be some dangers that could cause damage to it?

At one place the canal came to a river valley. The workers needed to build a dam across the river. How could they build a dam *and* get the canal across the valley?

Can you guess how they solved the problem?

They built a hollow dam! The canal flows through it!

At another place where the canal had to cross a valley, the workers built the aqueduct shown in this picture. Then they built a road above the canal.

Do some research in your school library on aqueducts. Are there any in Canada? Report back to your class on the location of some famous aqueducts in other parts of the world.

Much work had to be done to take the water to the fields. Here an aqueduct, or bridge, is being built to carry a branch canal across a wide valley. The water will flow between stone walls on the *top* of the aqueduct.

On the right stonemasons are chipping the blocks of stone to the right size. Then the blocks are carried to the hoists on shoulder poles. The hoists lift the stones up to the builders.

- How do the hoists work? (Imagine a pair of scales tipping up and down.)
- How are the arches of the aqueduct being built?
- How many different kinds of jobs do you see?
- How many teams of workers can you count?
- Why are aqueducts necessary?

Readying the fields for the water takes much hard work. The land must be levelled. Walls must be made to keep the water on the fields. It must not be allowed to run away. The levelled fields are called *terraces*. On steep slopes the terraces look like giant steps dug into the hillside.

The main grain crop grown in Linhsien County is wheat. Since the Red Flag Canal was built, there has been a regular supply of water. This has made it possible to grow rice. In this picture rice is growing on the terraced fields.

Some parts of western Canada also need water to grow crops. Where are they? What crops are grown there?

Irrigated Areas of Linhsien County

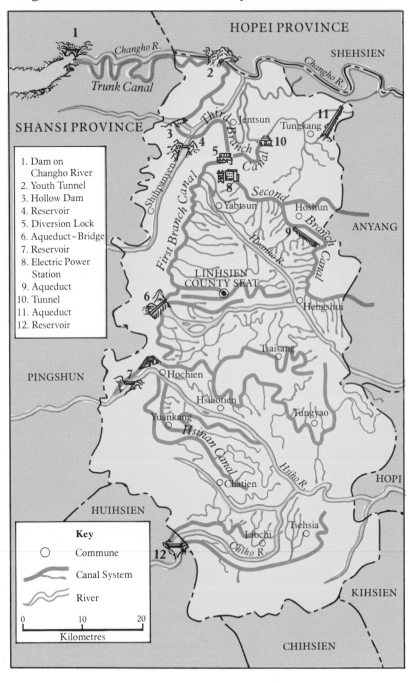

1. Dam on Changho River
2. Youth Tunnel
3. Hollow Dam
4. Reservoir
5. Diversion Lock
6. Aqueduct–Bridge
7. Reservoir
8. Electric Power Station
9. Aqueduct
10. Tunnel
11. Aqueduct
12. Reservoir

Key

○ Commune

〜 Canal System

〜 River

0   10   20
Kilometres

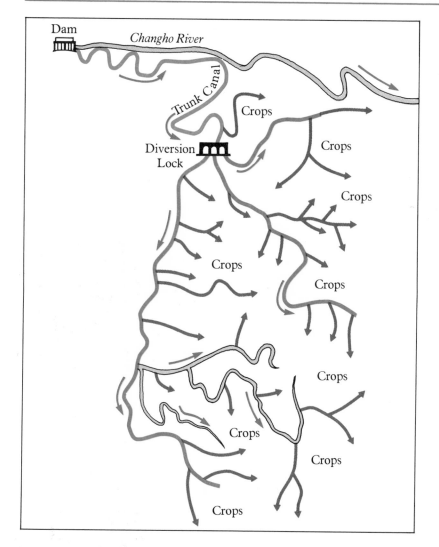

Dam

Changho River

Trunk Canal

Crops

Diversion
Lock

Crops

Crops

Crops

Crops

Crops

Crops

Crops

Crops

Crops

Crops

How the Water Reaches the Fields

Start at the dam on the Changho River. It is the highest point. Follow the arrows.

The *trunk* canal carries the water from the dam.

The diversion lock divides the water into *branch* canals.

Ditches carry the water from the branch canals into the fields to *irrigate* the crops.

Look at the map above. Note how the water reaches the fields from the trunk canal.

Now look at the map of the irrigated areas on page 38. Find the dam on the Changho River, the Youth Tunnel, the Hollow Dam, and the diversion lock. What would happen if these places were damaged and the water could not flow through the canal?

Compare this map with the one on page 27. What changes have been made to the land? How much land has been irrigated? To find out multiply the length of the irrigated land by its width (l x w). From north to south the distance is about 70 km (length). From east to west the distance is about 50 km (width). What is the answer in square kilometres?

What would be a similar area of land where you live?

Linhsien County Today

This corn will be used to feed pigs.
- What are these peasants doing?
- How can you tell that this field is terraced?

The peasants no longer fear droughts. The Red Flag Canal flows all year round, and water is stored in reservoirs. Fish have been put in storage ponds and are caught for food.

Many different crops are now grown in Linhsien County. Now that there is food for everyone, some land is used to grow cotton for clothing and other needs.

As more and more land was watered, the harvests got bigger and bigger. Year after year the peasants had bumper harvests.

When wheat is harvested, it is dried. These peasants are bagging the dried grain, weighing it, and then taking it away to be stored in a granary.

The communes in Linhsien County now grow more grain than they need. They sell it to other places in China that need it. With the money they earn in this way they can buy things they do not have. What might they buy?

Most of the work in the fields is done by teams of peasants working together. They also work together to lift and carry the heavy loads.

If trucks were available to carry the loads, what new skills would the workers have to learn?

Can you see the molten glass in this picture? The workers are making light bulbs. One worker is taking molten glass out of the furnace.

The peasants now enjoy better lives after their hard work building the canal and terracing the fields. They have time for other work. There are many new jobs. Water is used to make electricity, and most of the homes now have electric lights. Factories have been built to make electric motors and light bulbs. Machines are being made to help the peasants with their work in the fields. Houses are being built. The children have more time to go to school, and many schools have been built.

The woman in this picture is repairing a handle for a plough.

In the picture below, students are working in their schoolyard. Every day they do some work for the community in addition to their school work.

Before the canal was built, what work might the people in the pictures on pages 42 and 43 have been doing? What might the women have done? The men? The students?

The students are making mats and baskets. The day is hot and dry, but they are sitting comfortably in the shade of the trees. What does this tell you about the importance of the canal to their lives?

The picture above shows how bricks are made. How is this method different from the way in which bricks are made in Canada?

The women in the picture on the right are learning how a tractor works. They will soon use tractors in their fields.

Work on the canal still goes on. The water from the Changho River has silt in it. This silt would clog the canal if it were not cleaned out. The picture shows this being done.

The silt taken from the canal makes good soil. So, the peasants put it on their fields.

- How do you think the water was drained from the canal?
- What do you think caused the terrace wall to collapse?
- At what time of year is this most likely to happen?

These pictures show two of the ways in which people in Linhsien County spend their free time.

MEN AND MACHINES

At the same time as the Red Flag Canal was being built, a huge dam was under construction across the Peace River in northeastern British Columbia. Look for the Peace River and Hudson's Hope in your atlas. The dam is near Hudson's Hope and is called the W.A.C. Bennett Dam. It is one of the largest dams in the world. It is 180 m high and 2 km long. It took five years to build the dam. It was completed in 1968. The lake that formed behind the dam is over 300 km long. It is called Williston Lake. From the powerhouse inside the dam, power goes out to factories and homes in British Columbia.

The dam was made from gravel and sand that was found 7 km from the dam site. A 5 km conveyor belt was built to carry it to the site. Huge bulldozers with giant blades were used to bring the gravel and sand to the conveyor belt. At the dam site the gravel was sorted. Then belly-dump trucks, each carrying hundred-tonne loads, placed the gravel on the dam.

In both projects, the Red Flag Canal and the W.A.C. Bennett Dam, huge amounts of rock and rubble were moved. Water was taken to the fields of Linhsien County. Power was made for the factories and homes of British Columbia. The big difference between the two projects was in *how* they were done. Huge machines were used in building the dam. Huge numbers of workers were used in building the canal.

DANGER!

In many communities there are people who face dangers in their jobs. The upper picture shows two men working on the Red Flag Canal. They are swinging in space over the cliffs to dislodge loose rocks that might fall on their fellow workers when they start to drill into the cliffs. The lower picture shows a helicopter delivering supplies to an oil rig in Canada.

All these workers, including the helicopter pilot and those on the oil rig, are in some danger. Why do men and women do dangerous jobs? Should workers be exposed to dangers like these even if they are working for the good of other people?

Why didn't the people of Linhsien County use machines? We know that they didn't have any. They didn't have any money to hire machines, either. So they had to do the work themselves. This question is often faced by people when they have to do a project. Should they do the work themselves or find the money to hire men and machines to do it? The answer is never very simple.

Suppose your local community wants to make a new playground. Discuss whether the council should hire people and machines to do the work or call for volunteer help from the community. What would the problems be in each case?

3 Shanghai – Workers in a City

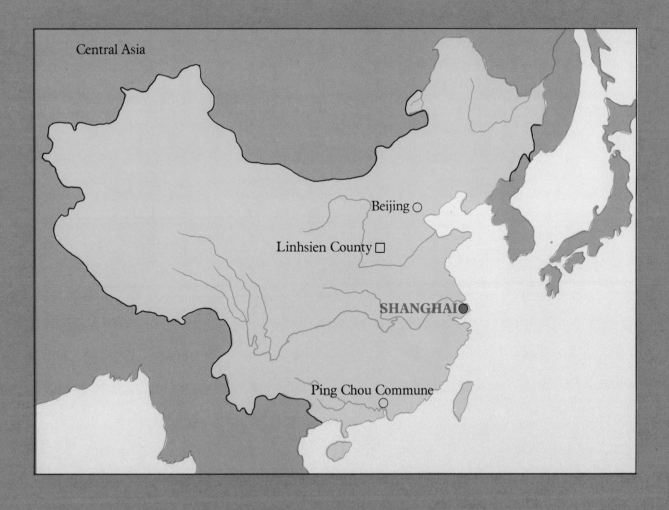

Central Asia

Beijing ○

Linhsien County □

SHANGHAI ●

Ping Chou Commune ○

Shanghai is one of the world's largest cities. About twelve million people live there. This is equal to about half of the people in all of Canada! Can you imagine so many people living in one city?

◄ Shanghai is located near the estuary of the Yangtze River, the most important waterway in China. It is the greatest industrial city in China. All kinds of goods are made in its factories. In its busy harbour ships from more than 100 countries of the world come to load and unload cargoes.

Shanghai has some tall office buildings. But most buildings are two- or three-storey apartment blocks or rows of houses. Homes often have only one or two rooms. Sometimes two or more families share a kitchen.

▼

How Shanghai Is Governed

Shanghai is very large. It includes the city itself and the surrounding farmland. How might such a large city be governed so that the people feel that they have a say in running it?

Shanghai is a municipality. It has one central government. The city is divided into districts, each with a district committee. Each district is divided into neighbourhoods. These are like the communes described in chapter 1. Each district has a neighbourhood committee. In each neighbourhood there are many residents' committees. Each of these represents about 600 or 700 households. The chart on this page shows these parts of Shanghai's government. The number of each part shown is not exact.

All the members of the residents' committees are elected. But

Government of Shanghai

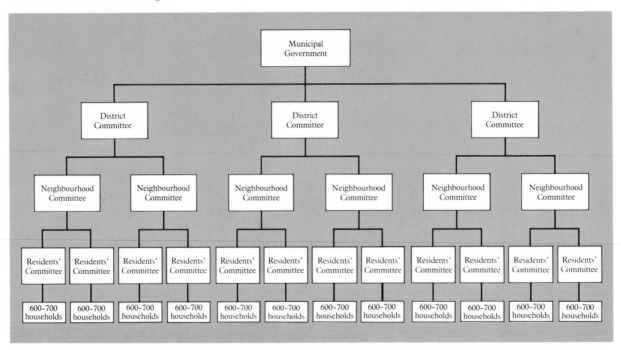

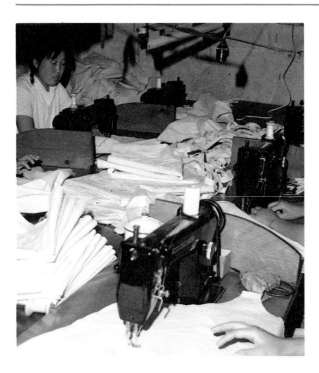

they must be approved by a government committee. In the neighbourhood committees some members are elected, and some are appointed by the government.

Each of the committees serves the people of Shanghai.

The municipal government is responsible for traffic control, public health, population records, the running of state factories, large public-works projects, and licences.

The district committees take care of local health services, telephones, water supply, drains, road repair, local traffic control, population records, and local licences.

The neighbourhood committees control the work of the residents' committees, explain new policies, hear complaints, and run small factories, some local services, clinics, schools, and housing.

The residents' committees carry out the instructions of the neighbourhood committees and make suggestions for improving the life and work of the householders.

The picture on the left shows a clothing factory in Shanghai. The two children in the picture on the right are playing in a park. If these pictures had been taken in Canada, would they have been any different?

This picture shows some typical Shanghai homes. For what purposes would the balconies be used by the people?

A Neighbourhood Community

The Tienshan workers live in an area that was set up in 1952 on the outskirts of Shanghai. Since then the area has expanded. Today 60 000 people live there in 15 000 households. Most of the residents are factory workers and their families.

Building houses and factories has been an important task for the neighbourhood committee. Most of the families live in two rooms, even in the new apartment blocks. The committee is always striving to provide better living conditions in the homes. For instance, it tries to improve the lighting and the kitchens, and to provide more space.

Residents do not own their own homes. Housing is controlled by the committee. Everyone is issued a permit to live in a specific house or apartment. The committee decides how much rent each family will pay. It also takes care of repairing broken electric wires and drains and damage to homes. When more water taps or drains are needed, the committee asks the district committee to supply them. Nothing is ever wasted in China. So the committee renovates old buildings rather than having them torn down.

Old housing in Shanghai. Compare this picture with the one on page 54. What differences are there between the older and newer buildings? What things are similar?

Crèche   Nursery school

The education and care of children are very important responsibilities for the neighbourhood committee. There are four middle schools (junior high schools), seven primary schools, and twelve kindergartens, nurseries, or crèches in the area.

Babies up to one-and-a-half years of age may be looked after in a crèche while their mothers are working. Grandparents also help take care of babies at home. Children go to kindergarten at age five, to primary school at age seven, and to middle school at age thirteen.

In what way is this school system different from or the same as the one in Canada?

Why do you think the Chinese consider education very important?

The Tienshan Neighbourhood Committee organizes many other services in addition to housing and education. It has built a library, swimming pool, cinema, and play centres for children and old people.

For many workers in small factories and for men and women helping in the community the midday meal is a welcome break. The committee runs several canteens that provide good, cheap meals. Some food, such as rice, is rationed. The committee issues ration coupons to the people who live and work in the area. The

Primary school   Middle school

Try to tell what kinds of food are being prepared. How many people do you think might eat in this canteen?

amount of food each person is allowed depends on his/her work. A worker in a steel plant would get more food than a teacher. Adults are allotted more food than children are.

Vegetables from outside the city are sold freely in street markets like the one shown here.

- How do you think these vegetables were brought into the city?

- How are the vegetables weighed?
- Do you recognize any of the vegetables?

The people in this picture work in a clinic. One of them is always there to provide drugs for sick people. Here, they are discussing treatment for a patient.

Health services have been developed. They are available to everyone. There are doctors or nurses at the many clinics in the area. Medical services are not costly. Workers pay only a few fen for drugs.

The committee takes care of the streets and housing areas. This sweeper is helping to prevent sickness by keeping the street clean.

Police officers and firefighters are employed by the municipal, or central, government. They work closely with the neighbourhood committee. The police are helped by the workers' militia. This group patrols the streets and helps to prevent crime.

There is very little stealing in China. It is honourable to report to the police anyone who does not obey the law.

The Tienshan Neighbourhood Committee has helped to develop many small industries. Goods are produced for local sale. Some factories make parts for large factories. Sometimes goods are produced by a few people working in a home. Most of the factories are small, and very simple machines are used.

The neighbourhood committee directs the workers to their jobs and decides how many work points they will earn. The work points determine the wages of the workers.

At all busy intersections police control traffic from shelters like this. People also come to the police for help and information. Discuss with other students whether there are any differences between the work of the police in China and in Canada and, if so, what they might be.

This shoemaker works at home. ►
What is he making? What
materials is he using?

These women are making fans in
a small factory where twenty
people are employed.
- What would the fans be used
  for?
- What kind of machinery
  would speed up the
  production?

▼

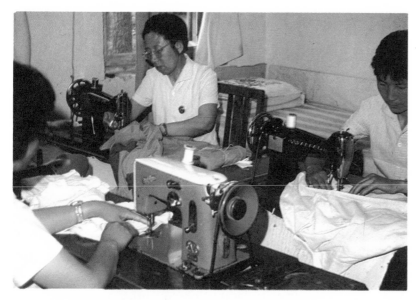

◄ These women are working in a room in an older type of house.
- What do you think they are making?
- How can you tell that this room is used for other purposes?
- Why do you think that this is so?

This worker is making furniture in a one-room factory.
- What do you think he is making?
- Why does he use old wood?
- Who will use the furniture?

▼

State-Owned Factories

There are two types of factories in China, the small neighbourhood one and the large state-owned factory. State-owned factories are planned and operated to benefit the whole country. Goods are produced for use within China and for sale to other countries. Machinery and fertilizer are made to support agriculture in China. Textiles are exported so that China can buy machinery and other products from foreign countries.

Iron, steel, coal, heavy machinery, textiles, and fertilizer plants are usually state owned and run. A management committee is set up in each factory. It makes the key decisions. There are always some Communist party members on the management committee. The workers are divided into workshops and production teams, which are like the brigades and teams on a commune. Workers elect the management committee and the workshop and

Compare the textile factory shown here and on page 65 with the small neighbourhood factories shown on pages 62 and 63. What are the main differences? Where would you prefer to work? Why?

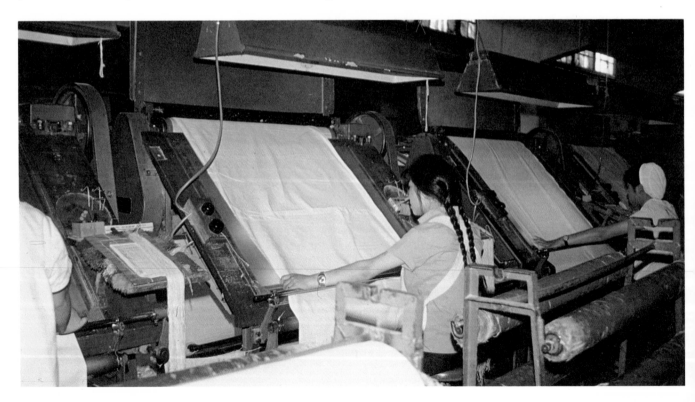

production-team leaders. The leaders allocate jobs, provide raw materials and tools, and look after safety in the factory.

When a worker is assigned to a job, he/she usually spends all of his/her working life at that job. There is almost no chance to move from one factory to another or from one city to another. Some workers may be promoted to workshop leader or factory manager. But they are still expected to do some of the tasks that ordinary workers do.

The factories operate seven days per week. Each worker works eight hours per day, six days per week. Every day one-seventh of the factory staff has a day off. There are no paid vacations, but everyone celebrates special days, such as New Year's Day, Spring Festival, and National Day.

Factory wages are paid once per month. Men and women are paid at the same rate. There are no profit-sharing or bonus payments. A beginning worker receives 35 yuan per month. The

The pictures here and on page 67 show an apartment being built, a courtyard of a new apartment, and the inside of one of the apartments. What differences and similarities can you see between these apartments and Canadian ones?

average worker earns 50 to 60 yuan, and a skilled worker earns 100 yuan. Workers do not pay income tax, and their health care is free. Members of a worker's family pay half of the cost of health care. Men retire at age 60, women at 55. They receive 80 per cent of their final salary as a pension.

To make it easier for women to be part of the work force, the management committee provides household service shops. These shops do washing, mending, and sewing. The committee owns canteens which offer cheap but wholesome lunches and dinners. Most families can afford to eat out several times per week. There are no frozen or canned foods. So, food must be purchased every day. Often older people in the family shop for the fresh vegetables and fish that are brought to the city from the rural communes around the city.

Babies and preschool children may be cared for in a nursery run by the factory. Factories run primary and sometimes secondary schools too. Students are also expected to be workers. They clean the school rooms and grounds. They often make small parts that the factory uses.

Most state factories build modern high-rise apartments for their workers. This kind of apartment rents for 3.10 yuan per month. The electricity costs 1.00 yuan and the water 0.70 yuan per month.

A couple and their two children would live in a one- or two-room apartment. Some families have a grandparent living with

An old street in Shanghai

them as well. Because China has such a large population, the government is very strict about how many children families should have. People are discouraged from having more than two children.

Some families live in older houses. These homes do not always have running water, and families may share an outdoor toilet. Cooking is done outdoors on a barbecue-like stove. The fuel is a mixture of dried mud and coal dust. People often eat outside while they chat with their neighbours.

What People Do in Their Spare Time

Life in China is not all work. When people in Shanghai have leisure time, they might visit one of the many beautiful parks, gardens, or temples. There is usually a boating pond and a teahouse to enjoy. Several of the old temples and palaces have

This garden is as popular with tourists as it is with the Chinese themselves.

been turned into museums. Cinemas and theatres offer performances that show people examples of good conduct. Restaurants serve food that looks good, smells good, and tastes good. The prices are low enough to suit the budgets of most families.

Children from seven to seventeen years of age may go to the Children's Palace. There they may learn ballet, music, art, drama, handicrafts, and mechanics. The children make such things as car filters, electronic parts, school equipment, and embroidery.

China displays the things that are manufactured by the state factories at the Industrial Exhibition in Shanghai. Buyers and tourists can see what is available for sale. Workers can look at the

There are many restaurants in Shanghai.

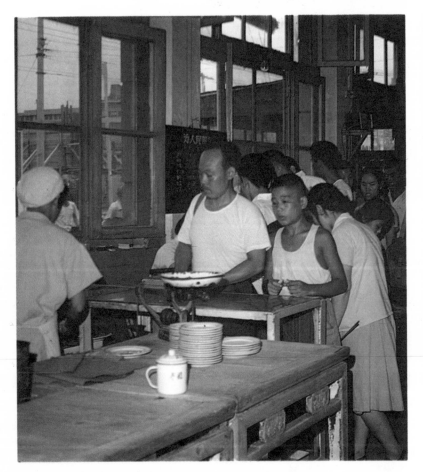

These pictures were taken at the Children's Palace. What are the children learning to do?

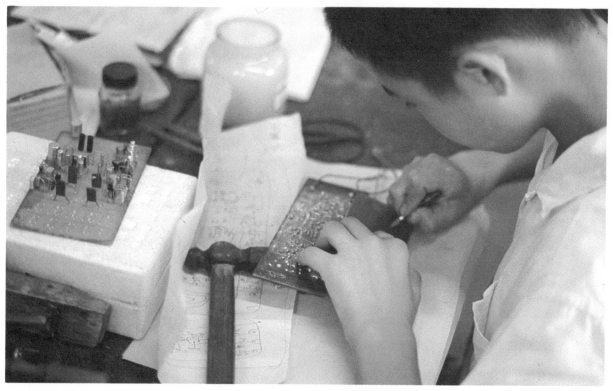

Visitors from all over the world come to Shanghai to see demonstrations of products such as these at the Industrial Exhibition. Are there any similar exhibitions where you live?

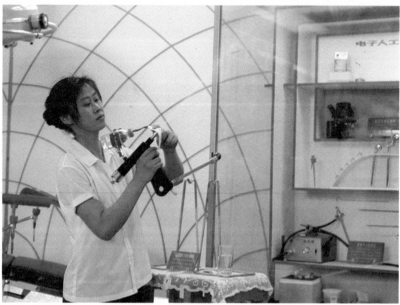

products from other factories, too. There are many different products on display.

Sports are very popular with everyone. People of all ages exercise every day. Tai Chi is a special form of exercise and meditation that is done each morning. Even the oldest citizens participate in Tai Chi.

Young and old enjoy table tennis, basketball, swimming, shadow

These artists at the Research Art Institute are trying to design decorative products. When the products are finished, they will be produced in factories and sold all over the world. Many people come to watch these artists at work.

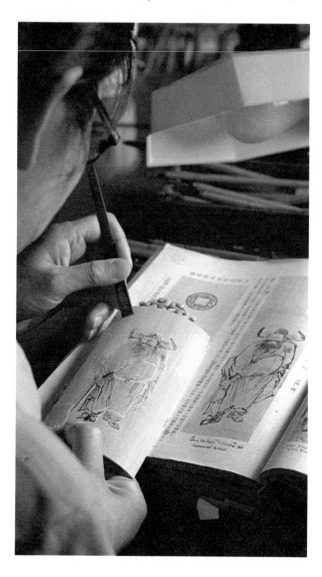

Do you do any of these activities in your spare time? Where do you do them? Why do you think the Chinese usually do them outside?

boxing, and card games. Hopscotch, skipping, and marbles are the children's favourites. What sports do you play? What are your leisure activities? How are they different from the sports and pastimes in China? How can you explain the differences?

4 Beijing
– The Capital

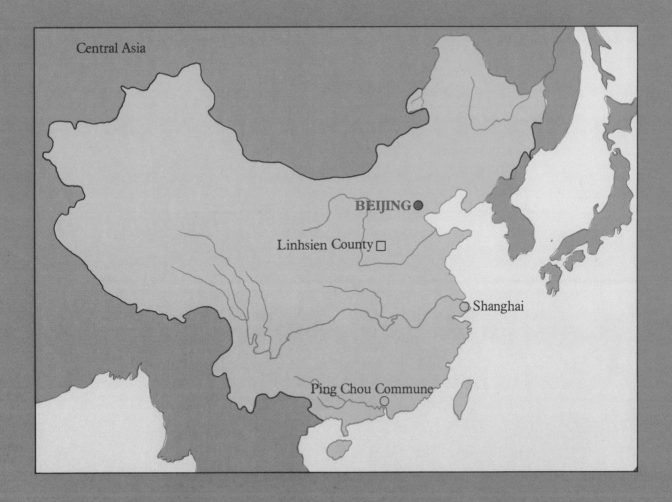

Central Asia

BEIJING●

Linhsien County □

○ Shanghai

Ping Chou Commune ○

A Mixture of New and Old

Beijing is the capital city of the People's Republic of China. It is a large city. There are over nine million people living in Beijing.

Beijing is an old city. It began as a trading centre about 2500 years ago. At that time it was called Peiking, meaning "northern capital". It became a capital city in about 400 B.C. In A.D. 905 the name was changed to Yenching by invaders from Manchuria. Later, a Mongol leader, Kublai Khan, made it his capital city and changed the name back to Peiking. In the 1300s the Ming rulers called it Peiping, which means "northern peace". Later they changed the city's name

Entrance to the Forbidden City

to Peiking. The name remained Peiking until the government of the People's Republic of China changed it to Beijing in 1980.

The municipality of Beijing is made up of the old city, newer suburbs, and the surrounding farmland. The old city was once surrounded by walls. Many of these have been torn down. Inside this section are the palaces and temples of the emperors of old China. This part of Beijing is called the Forbidden City, because long ago only the emperor's family and servants could enter it. Today the palaces are museums that are open to everyone.

A temple at the Summer Palace Gardens, just outside Beijing

Tien An Men Square in Beijing

Surrounding the Forbidden City is the Imperial City. It contains parks, lakes, and the homes of the Chinese Communist leaders. The southern entrance to the Imperial City is called Tien An Men or the Gate of Heavenly Peace. The gate overlooks a huge square where celebrations of national holidays take place. There are parades and fireworks. The government leaders speak to the people in the square from a balcony on the gate.

The Great Hall of the People, China's parliament building, is on the south side of the square. Once every five years over 3000 delegates to the National People's Congress meet in the hall. State banquets and receptions for foreign visitors are held here as well.

The city of Beijing is China's cultural centre as well as its capital. Students from all parts of China come to attend college, university, or technical school in Beijing. The Beijing library is the largest in China. There are more than twenty-five theatres in the city. Many of China's publishing houses are located in Beijing. The Beijing Opera Company performs operas about the Communist revolution

May 1 is an important holiday for workers in China. This picture shows a May Day celebration in Beijing.

Many factories such as these in Beijing have been built in China in the last thirty years.

all over China. Artists carve jade and ivory and paint scenes of the way of life in the People's Republic of China.

Today Beijing is an industrial city. The government built factories to produce chemicals, iron and steel, farm machinery, electronic equipment, and textiles. Coal is mined near the city for use in the steel industry. The mines and factories are owned and run by the government. Porcelain, tapestries, and tiles are made in Beijing by craftspeople who work in state-owned factories.

The city combines the ancient and the modern. This is most obvious in the architecture. The buildings in the old city are much richer in colour and ornamentation than those in the newer areas. Buildings constructed under the Communist government are more like those in Western nations.

These pictures at the Temple of Heaven in Beijing show the high quality of Chinese arts and crafts.

These farmers are bringing their produce to market in Beijing.

There are agricultural communes in the municipality of Beijing. Farmers grow grain, vegetables, fruit, and cotton. Much of their produce is used by the people in the city. Ducks, pigs, and sheep are raised to supply meat for Beijing families. Some of these are raised on the farmers' private plots. Each farmer keeps the money received from the sale of such produce and livestock.

The Chinese Government

In China all the power to make laws is held by one level of government. The central government is controlled by the Communist party.

China is divided into provinces, counties, and districts. Each of these levels elects members to its own People's Congress. Provincial, county, or district congresses have no power to make laws or set policies. Only the National People's Congress can do that. The People's Congress at each of the lower levels can only carry out the policies and programs set by the central government.

A Brief Look at China's Long History

Many historians think that China is one of the places where civilization began. For many centuries China was ruled by a series of emperors. The people obeyed the emperor because they thought that he was the "son of heaven". They believed that God had given him the right to rule the earth. He was expected to rule the country well. If things went wrong, the people withdrew their belief in him as the "son of heaven", and sometimes a revolution occurred. Then, a new emperor, or *dynasty,* took over.

The affairs of the country were managed by officials called *mandarins.* They collected the taxes and carried out the wishes of whichever emperor was in power. To get a mandarin's position, a person had to pass an examination based on the ideas of a man named Confucius. Confucianism taught that citizens should be loyal to the emperor and honour those older than themselves. Mandarins usually came from wealthy families. Peasant families could not afford to support a son long enough for him to learn the necessary information.

The emperors had the right to do almost anything they wished with their subjects or their property. There were many people who had no rights at all. Women and children had a very low place in society.

Chinese scholars made many discoveries in astronomy, geometry, and the arts. They invented gunpowder, the compass, paper, and a printing process. The manufacture of silk and porcelain was begun. Craftspeople became skilled in fabric dyeing and metal casting.

For hundreds of years Chinese civilization grew in its own way. There was very little contact with the rest of the world. An Italian trader, Marco Polo, came to China during the reign of Kublai Khan in the 1200s. He told stories of the riches of China when he returned home. But European traders did not greatly affect life in China until the nineteenth century.

At that time Great Britain and France forced China to let their missionaries into the country and to allow them to open the coastal cities to trade. Later, other European countries obtained trading ports. Foreigners began to live in Beijing. Many Chinese resented

One impressive accomplishment of the ancient Chinese was the building of the Great Wall. The early rulers of China feared an invasion from the people to the north. They built walls across the tops of the mountains to protect themselves.

The emperor Chin Shih Huang Ti had all these walls joined together to form the Great Wall. The wall curves and loops across three provinces. It crosses the highest mountains. All of the materials needed to build the wall had to be carried to the top of the mountains.

The wall is built on a bed of wide, square stones. There are many one- or two-storey towers along the length of the wall. Thousands of peasants were taken from their farms to work on the wall. So many were killed or died during the work that people began to call it the great burial wall.

Emperors often came from the same family or dynasty. One of the longest-lasting was the Ming Dynasty. It built huge tombs. The road to the tombs was guarded by stone animal and human figures. Some of these are shown in this picture. Many treasures were buried with the emperors. These tombs have now been opened, and the art treasures are on display.

this. There was an uprising against the foreigners in 1900, but the Chinese were defeated.

Finally, in 1911, the long rule of the emperors came to an end. Following a revolution, Dr. Sun Yat-sen was proclaimed president of a new Republic of China. But within a short time China was taken over by several local rulers called *warlords*. There was unrest and fighting among the regions of China for many years.

In 1928 the Chinese Nationalist Party gained control of part of the country. During the Second World War Japan captured much of China's territory. The Chinese Nationalists regained control in 1945. But in 1949 the Chinese Communists gained control of most of the country. They set up the People's Republic of China.

Glossary

advanced co-operative	An organization of land and peasants that developed into communes.
aqueduct	A bridge to support a channel to carry water across a valley.
brigade	A group of peasants organized by a committee in a commune. A brigade is made up of many production teams.
cadre	A worker or peasant who helps the Communist party. He/she is usually a member of a committee.
commune	An organization of land, villages, and factories run by a committee. Rural China is divided into communes.
crèche	A day nursery for babies and small children.
diversion lock	A place where a canal is divided into smaller canals.
drought	A long period without rain.
dynasty	A line of rulers from the same family.
estuary	The wide mouth of a river.
fen	A unit of money in China; 100 fen = 1 yuan.
latitude	The distance north or south of the equator, measured in degrees.
monsoon	The rainy season.
pension	Money paid regularly to people after they have retired from work.
precipitation	The amount of rain and snow that falls on the land.
ration coupons	A piece of paper that can be exchanged for a fixed amount of food or goods.
reservoir	A lake made by people and used to store water.
sampan	A small, flat-bottomed boat which is widely used on the waterways of China.
threshing	Beating out the grain from the husk.
work points	Awards for work. In parts of China a worker's wages are paid according to the number of work points earned.
yuan	The main unit of money in China.